THE LITER

AN EARLY METRIC BOOK

THE LITER

by WILLIAM J. SHIMEK

pictures by George Overlie

 Lerner Publications Company • Minneapolis

In the Early Metric books, we have used the "er" spellings of "meter" and "liter" in order that young readers may easily recognize and pronounce these words. The "re" spellings of the metric measurements—"metre," "litre," "kilometre"—are, of course, also correct and are commonly used in other countries. Reports issued by the U. S. Office of Education indicate the possibility that the United States will eventually adopt the "re" forms of these words.

LIBRARY OF CONGRESS CATALOGING IN PUBLICATION DATA

Shimek, William J.
    The liter.

    (An Early Metric Book)
    SUMMARY: A simple introduction to the liter, the metrical unit of volume or capacity.

    1. Metric system—Juvenile literature. [1. Metric system] I. Overlie, George, ill. II. Title.

QC92.5.S47 1975   389'.152   74.11895
ISBN 0-8225-0587-8

Published simultaneously in Canada by J. M. Dent & Sons (Canada) Ltd., Don Mills, Ontario.

Manufactured in the United States of America.

International Standard Book Number: 0-8225-0587-8
Library of Congress Catalog Card Number: 74-11895

Second Printing 1976

How much water is in this glass?

How much gasoline will the tank of this car hold?

What is the capacity of a milk carton?

How much water does a swimming pool hold?

To measure
how much
something
will hold . . .
use the

LITER

To measure
volume or
capacity . . .
use the

LITER

Small volumes are often measured with the . . .

MILLIliter.

Soupspoon—
10 milliliters

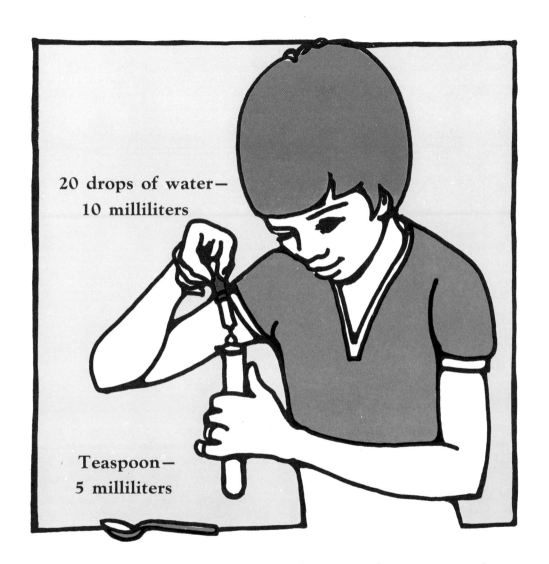

20 drops of water—
10 milliliters

Teaspoon—
5 milliliters

Here are some volumes that can be measured
with the milliliter.

Small volumes can also be measured with the . . .

CENTIliter.

Here are some volumes that can be measured with the centiliter.

Bottle of pop—about 40 centiliters

Coffee cup—
about 20 centiliters

A CENTILITER

has the same volume as

10

MILLILITERS.

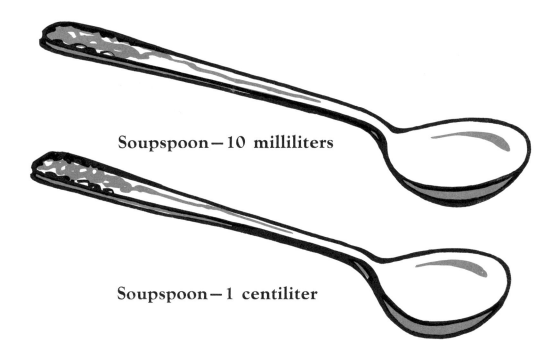

Soupspoon—10 milliliters

Soupspoon—1 centiliter

Many volumes can be measured with either

the CENTILITER

or

the MILLILITER.

Some volumes are measured with the ...

DECIliter.

Bottle of pop—
about 4 deciliters

Coffee cup—
about 2 deciliters

Here are some volumes that can be measured
with the deciliter.

A DECILITER

has the same volume as

10

CENTILITERS.

1 soupspoon—1 centiliter

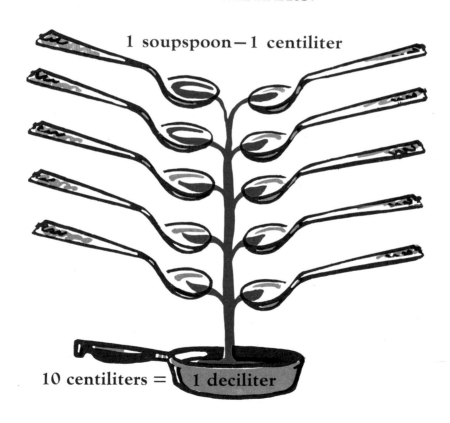

10 centiliters = 1 deciliter

A DECILITER

has the same volume as

100

MILLILITERS.

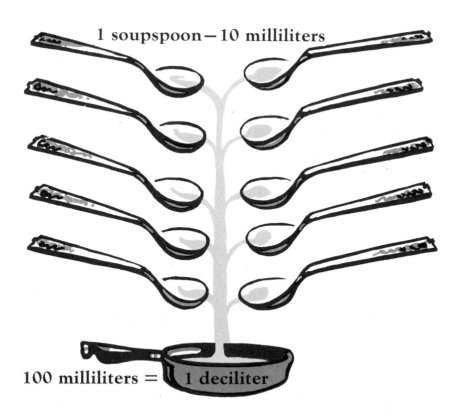

1 soupspoon — 10 milliliters

100 milliliters = 1 deciliter

Many volumes can be measured with either

DECILITERS

or

CENTILITERS

or

MILLILITERS.

Pretend that you have a box that will hold exactly 1000 milliliters. The box might look like this:

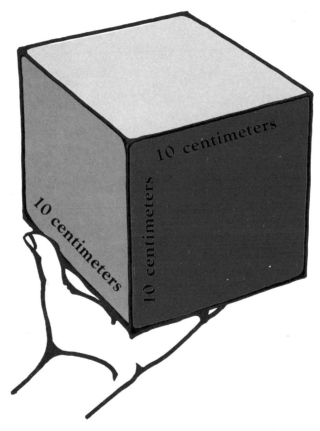

The volume of this box has a very special name.

It is called a LITER.

Every liter has the same volume as

1000 MILLILITERS

or

100 CENTILITERS

or

10 DECILITERS.

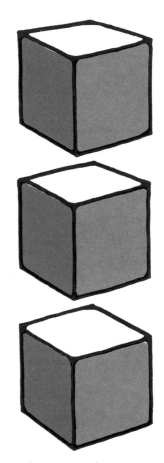

Ask your parents or your teacher to show you a container that will hold a liter. Look at it. Hold it in your hand.

Many volumes can be measured with the liter.

The volume of a carton of milk is about 1 liter.

The volume of a large bottle of pop is about 1 liter.

A small can of paint will hold about 1 liter. Larger paint cans hold about 4 liters.

The volume of a motorcycle gas tank is about 10 liters.

Ten liters is called a DEKAliter.

The volume of a motorcycle gas tank is about 1 dekaliter.

The volume of the gas tank on some large cars is about 100 liters.

One hundred liters is called a HECTOliter.

The volume of the gas tank on some large cars is about 1 hectoliter.

The volume of a large propane tank is about 1000 liters. This would be the same size as a tank that is 1 meter long and 1 meter wide and 1 meter high.

One thousand liters is called a KILOliter.

The volume of a large propane tank is about 1 kiloliter.

A swimming pool may hold as much as 7500 kiloliters of water.

The volume of air in the Houston Astrodome is about 2,000,000 kiloliters.

The name of each of the measures in this book has a shorter form.

KILOLITER ▶ KL

HECTOLITER ▶ HL

DEKALITER ▶ DAL

LITER ▶ L

DECILITER ▶ DL

CENTILITER ▶ CL

MILLILITER ▶ ML

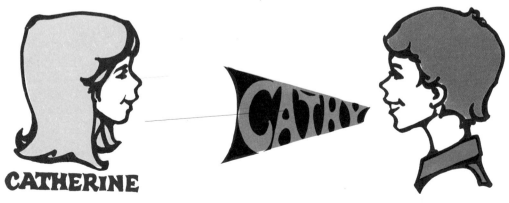

CATHERINE ▶ CATHY

10 MILLILITERS (ML) = 1 CENTILITER (CL)
100 MILLILITERS (ML) = 1 DECILITER (DL)
1000 MILLILITERS (ML) = 1 LITER (L)

10 CENTILITERS (CL) = 1 DECILITER (DL)
100 CENTILITERS (CL) = 1 LITER (L)

10 DECILITERS (DL) = 1 LITER (L)

10 LITERS (L) = 1 DEKALITER (DAL)
100 LITERS (L) = 1 HECTOLITER (HL)
1000 LITERS (L) = 1 KILOLITER (KL)

10 DEKALITERS (DAL) = 1 HECTOLITER (HL)
100 DEKALITERS (DAL) = 1 KILOLITER (KL)

10 HECTOLITERS (HL) = 1 KILOLITER (KL)

ABOUT THE SPECIAL WORDS USED IN THIS BOOK

Volume is a word used to describe the space that an object occupies or encloses. Capacity (kuh-PASS-uh-tee) means "the amount of material that a container can hold."

ABOUT THE AUTHOR

William J. Shimek has taught mathematics for many years in the public schools of Minnesota. He has made good use of his extensive classroom experience as well as his knowledge of mathematics in writing this series of metric books for young readers. A native of Minnesota, Mr. Shimek received a master's degree in math education from Florida State University in 1972. Since 1961, he has taught mathematics at Brooklyn Center Junior-Senior High School in Brooklyn Center, Minnesota. In addition to his activities in professional organizations such as the National Council of Teachers of Mathematics, Mr. Shimek devotes his spare time to an unusual hobby—distance running—and to long bicycle trips with his family. He has also found time to write a math book for young readers entitled PATTERNS: WHAT ARE THEY? Mr. Shimek lives in Blaine, Minnesota, with his wife and four children.